Greek Mythology

The Ultimate Beginner's Guide to Jump into the Myths of Greek Gods, Goddesses and Heroes

By

Philip Walove

© Copyright 2023 by Philip Walove - All rights reserved.

This document is geared towards providing exact and reliable information in regards to the topic and issue covered. The publication is sold with the idea that the publisher is not required to render accounting, officially permitted, or otherwise, qualified services. If advice is necessary, legal or professional, a practiced individual in the profession should be ordered.

- From a Declaration of Principles, which was accepted and approved equally by a Committee of the American Bar Association and a Committee of Publishers and Associations.

In no way is it legal to reproduce, duplicate, or transmit any part of this document in either electronic means or in printed format. Recording of this publication is strictly prohibited, and any storage of this document is not allowed unless with written permission from the publisher. All rights reserved.

The information provided herein is stated to be truthful and consistent, in that any liability, in terms of inattention or otherwise, by any usage or abuse of any policies, processes, or directions contained within is the solitary and utter responsibility of the recipient reader. Under no circumstances will any legal responsibility or blame be held against the publisher for any reparation, damages, or monetary loss due to the information herein, either directly or indirectly.

Respective authors own all copyrights not held by the publisher.

The information herein is offered for informational purposes solely and is universal as so. The presentation of the information is without a contract or any type of guarantee assurance.

The trademarks that are used are without any consent, and the publication of the trademark is without permission or backing by the trademark owner. All trademarks and brands within this book are for clarifying purposes only and are owned by the owners themselves, not affiliated with this document.

Table of Contents

Introduction 7

Chapter 1 Greek Mythology 11

   1.1 The Greek Creation Myth 12

   1.2 The Creation Myth: Gods and Titans 12

   1.3 Gods, Heroes, Mortals, and Monsters 14

   1.4 Deities 15

Chapter 2 The Olympians 19

Chapter 3 Greek Gods 21

   3.1 Zeus: God of the Sky 21

   3.2 Poseidon: God of the Sea 23

   3.3 Hades: God of the Underworld and Wealth; God and King of the Dead 24

   3.4 Apollo: God of Music, Prophecy, Healing and Plague 26

   3.5 Hephaestus: God of Fire, Craftsmanship, and Sculpture 28

   3.6 Ares: God of War, Courage, and Civil Order 29

   3.7 Hermes: God of Herds and Flocks, Travelers, Trade, Writing, Athleticism, and Astronomy; the Messenger God 30

   3.8 Dionysus: God of Theater, Wine, Vegetation, Pleasure, and Madness 31

Chapter 4 Greek Goddess 33

   4.1 Hestia: Goddess of the Hearth and Home 33

   4.2 Persephone: Goddess of Vegetation, Spring and the underworld 34

   4.3 Hecate: Goddess of Magic, witchcraft, Ghosts, and Necromancy 36

4.4 Cerberus: Guardian of the underworld 37

4.5 Demeter: Goddess of Agriculture and the Harvest 39

4.6 Hera: Goddess of Marriage, Woman, and Fertility; Queen of the Gods 41

4.7 Athena: Goddess of Strategic War and Wisdom 43

4.8 Aphrodite: Goddess of Love, Beauty, and Sex 44

4.9 Artemis: Goddess of the Hunt and Wilderness 46

Chapter 5 Deities 48

5.1 Prometheus: A Titan; God of Forethought 49

5.2 Pandora: The First Woman 50

5.3 Leto: A Titan; Goddess of Motherhood; Protector of the Young 52

5.4 Daphne: A Nymph 55

5.5 Eros: God of Erotic Love and Sex 56

5.6 Psyche: A Princess; Later, the Goddess of the Soul 57

5.7 Echo and Narcissus: A Nymph and a Young Mortal Man (the Son of a River God and a Nymph) 58

5.8 Typhon and Echidna 59

Chapter 6 Heroes and Mortals 62

6.1 Semele: A Princess of Thebes; Daughter of Cadmus and Harmonia 63

6.2 Io: A Princess of Argos 64

6.3 Europa: A Phoenician Princess 65

6.4 Leda: A Queen of Sparta; Mother of Castor, Polydeuces, Helen, and Clytemnestra 66

6.5 Actaeon: A Shepherd and Hunter of Boeotia 67

6.6 Theseus: A Hero and Prince of Athens 68

6.7 Hippolyta: An Amazonian Queen 69

6.8 *Ariadne and Phaedra: Princess of Crete; Goddess and Wife of Dionysus; Wife of Theseus* 72

6.9 *Heracles: A Hero of Thebes; Son of Zeus* 74

6.10 *Perseus: A Hero; Son of Zeus* 77

6.11 *Medusa: A Gorgon* 78

6.12 *Jason: A Hero and Prince of Iolchus* 80

6.13 *Medea: A Witch; Daughter of Aeëtes; Granddaughter of the Titan Helios* 81

6.14 *Cadmus: A Hero; Founder of Thebes; a Prince of the Phoenicians* 82

6.15 *Atalanta: A Heroine of Arcadia* 83

6.16 *Daedalus: An Inventor from Athens* 84

6.17 *Icarus: The Son of Daedalus* 85

6.18 *Pasiphaë and Minos: A Queen and King of Knossos, Crete* 87

6.19 *Minotaur: A Monstrous Half-Man, Half Bull* 88

6.20 *Orpheus and Eurydice: A Young Musician and a Beautiful Young Woman* 90

Conclusion 91

Introduction

Since the beginning of human history, people have felt the need to provide explanations for the mysteries and wonders of the planet: oceans and the mountains, earthquakes, the changing seasons, storms, floods and volcanoes, and the presence of creatures, including humans. Early people in every civilization on Earth produced supernatural creatures and gods to explain these events and give solace and guidance. Tribes migrated from one area to another as time passed and split up, regrouped, grew in number, and relocated to other territories; they carried their legends with them. As the tales were handed down, they adapted to the climate, people's language, and folklore. People eventually constructed temples and shrines for their heroes and gods. They prayed to them for assistance, offered sacrifices, and held festivals in their honor. In certain nations, like Rome, kings assumed the position of gods. There are temples dedicated to Athene, Zeus, Aphrodite, and other goddesses and gods throughout Greece. Their names live on in place names, people's names, and history since the people who worshiped the divinities were certain they had once walked the Earth.

In the original mythology of most societies, female deities held the position of the supreme deity. The EARTH MOTHER was responsible for the origin of all new life. She was a goddess who oversaw the heavens, the seasons, and the harvests, and she was also known as the moon or the sun. Throughout many ages, it was eventually determined by humanity that both the male and the female were required for the successful reproduction of the species. The Moon Goddess and the Earth Mother were eventually supplanted by masculine sun and sky gods, often represented by rams or bulls. In Greek tales, the behavior of Zeus toward his sister-wife, Hera, is a paradigmatic example of the demise of the royal mother. He was a very unfaithful, disrespectful, and naughty spouse all at the same time. His dalliances and Hera's rage may exemplify the orthodox religious sentiment (illustrated by Hera) against weddings or other associations (those of Zeus) between the nymphs and moon priestesses, and new Hellenic chieftains. This feeling is opposed to marriages or other liaisons between the two groups. This feeling is opposed to marriages or other liaisons between the new Hellenic chieftains and Zeus.

Greek mythology dates back a very long time. In the year 21st Century, the country that is known as Greece was the site of devotion dedicated to the Great Mother. An early version of worship of sky gods, Aryan, and the Indo-European language, were carried over by early conquerors from Asia Minor. They made their homes in the Central part of Greece and Thessaly, where they lived in harmony with the locals and married them. Homer referred to the subsequent waves of northern tribes as the Dorians and Achaeans. These waves were more destructive and hostile than the previous ones. These individuals did not value peace in any way. They suppressed the whole indigenous population of Sparta, which was located in the south region of Peloponnesus, and put them to work doing menial jobs. Helot was the name that the Achaeans gave to these slaves. The language of the Achaeans was a variation of an early Greek, and their writing system was an early form of what modern researchers refer to as Linear B.

The island of Crete, which is situated in the southern region of Greece, was so far a thriving civilization when the ravages and barbarians inhabited the region that we now name Greece Crete has been engaged in a commercial exchange with the far more primitive civilizations that may be found in Egypt and Asia even since ancient times. The civilization of Minoan achieved its pinnacle about the 17th Century and was recognized by that name at the time. After the fall of the Minoan civilization around the 15th Century, which was most likely brought on by a natural occurrence such as an upheaval, the Greeks took control of Crete.

The origins of the Greek tales can be traced back to many different parts of the primitive Balkan Peninsula, including Mycenae Boeotia, Attica Thrace, Argos, and the Peloponnesus, as well as many islands, Crete being one of them, as well as Asia

Minors and other places that are somewhat farther away, such as Sumer and Babylon. Homer, whose poems may have been written by numerous poets between 700 and 750 Before Christ, is regarded as the "ultimate origin" of the tales that come from Greece.

Chapter 1 Greek Mythology

Greeks were the first to construct gods and goddesses that resembled human beings: attractive men and women, elderly people with wit and dignity, and marvelously realistic animals (as well as a few monsters). The human condition served as the inspiration for all creative endeavors and philosophical inquiries in ancient Greece.

The gods and goddesses of Greek mythology often had interactions with humanity in locales that still exist today, such as cities and countries: Mount Ida, located on the Greek island of Crete, is said to have been the home of the god Zeus when he was growing up. The city of Thebes was where the legendary hero Heracles resided. It is possible to pinpoint the location near the island of Cythera, where the goddess Aphrodite is said to have emerged from the water.

Heroes in Greek mythology were able to triumph over their foes thanks to their cunning and cleverness. ODYSSEUS, for example, was supposed to have conceived of the wooden Trojan horse, in which the invading Greek warriors were concealed. Greek intelligence included a great deal more than just astute planning. The ancient Greeks were keen to learn as much as possible about themselves and the world around them.

1.1 The Greek Creation Myth

There is a certain degree of similarity between the various creation myths that can be found worldwide. These myths investigate early humans' efforts to explain the origin of the Earth, the Sun, the Moon, the stars, and the creatures that live on Earth, including men and women.

Hesiod's version of the creation story is often considered the most famous of all Greek myths (sometime around 800 B.C., after Homer). It talks of the initial CHAOS, a whirling mass without form, from which Mother Earth, GAIA, and her son-consort, URANUS, the sky, emerged. These two were responsible for developing all the Earth's creatures and flora. They were also responsible for creating the TITANS, the CYCLOPES with just one eye, and other atrocities that Uranus imprisoned underground.

In the end, Cronus, Uranus's son, succeeded him as ruler of the solar system. Cronus and Rhea were the parents of the twelve children who would become the Olympians, the most powerful gods and goddesses in Greek mythology.

1.2 The Creation Myth: Gods and Titans

According to Greek mythology, the universe first existed as a formless substance called Chaos, from which Gaia eventually emerged. Gaia was the personification of the Earth itself and was also known as Mother Earth. She immediately had a case of the lonesomes and fabricated a spouse for herself, Ouranos (yes, like Uranus, the planet). Together, they gave birth to:

- The Titans: The Titans are a group extremely similar to the gods; they are humanlike, and the main difference between them is their name and general prominence in mythology; nevertheless, they are also referred to as gods at times.

- The Hecatonchires: The Hecatonchires are a fantastic race of creatures, although they aren't spoken about very much. Each Hecatonchire has one hundred hands and fifty heads.

Kronos, one of the Titans, had a ravenous appetite for power and an obsessive desire to topple the gods who stood above him in the hierarchy of deities. Kronos dismembered his father, Ouranos, and then hurled the bodily pieces he had taken from his father into the ocean after he had castrated his father. Two distinct kinds of living things came into being as a result of the dropping blood droplets:

- The Erinyes: The Erinyes, also known as the Furies, were a group of three female monsters whose only purpose in life was to exact vengeance on people who disobeyed the natural rules of the Earth.

- The Gigantes: The Gigantes are a race of enormous, murderous monsters.

1.3 Gods, Heroes, Mortals, and Monsters

Although the Olympians had the highest prestige among the Greek pantheon, there were hundreds of additional gods and goddesses. The term "deities" is used widely to refer to these godlike figures who seemed to be human but were, strictly speaking, neither gods nor humans. Quite a few of the mythological figures from Greek literature fit this description.

Titans that weren't locked up with Kronos, including Prometheus and Epimetheus, and other great and lesser gods with significant backstories, like Eros, played a role (Cupid). Heroic figures (like Perseus, Heracles, Cadmus, and many more!) existed, some of whom were demigods' offspring, and others were only mortals. Even if their tales don't include the Olympians directly (though they typically do), they are nevertheless significant and spectacular tales in their own right.

Then comes the monsters. Among the most memorable characters in Greek mythology are the beasts and monsters who aren't human: Everyone is familiar with the stories of the Cyclopes and the multi-headed Hydra. Typhon and Echidna, two primordial monsters, produced many of the most infamous and terrible creatures of Greek mythology (more on those two in their entry).

1.4 Deities

1) Nymphs were lesser deities who were often linked to certain natural phenomena. Many different kinds of nymphs existed, classified according to their habitats and the causes to which they were most committed. Typically, you'd see these nymph types:

a) Naids: Naiads were nymphs of streams, rivers, and other freshwater sources. Yes, it seems odd that Oceanids were freshwater nymphs, but they were the descendants of the Titan Oceanus, the embodiment of the huge river that the Greeks thought ringed the planet.

b) The Dryads and Hamadryads: The Dryads and Hamadryads were woodland nymphs whose duty was to guard the forest's trees. The nymphs known as Hamadryads are distinguished from the Dryads by their undying loyalty to a particular tree.

c) The Hesperides: The Hesperides were a group of nymphs associated with the evening sky. They were the offspring of the Titan Hesperis. They watched over the Hesperides' Garden, where the legendary golden apples were grown.

d) Nereids: Among the Titans and sea gods, Nereus' daughters were known as Nereids.

e) Lampades: Underworld nymphs were called Lampades. The goddesses Persephone and Hecate had them carry torches as they traveled through Hades.

2) In ancient Greece, the nine Muses (Musae in Latin and Mousai in Greek) were the creative force behind all the great works of art, poetry, and drama. Zeus and Mnemosyne, Titan goddess of memory, had two daughters whom they named after themselves. Calliope was the muse of epic poetry, Thalia of comedy, Euterpe of lyrical poetry, Terpsichore of dance and choral singing, Polyhymnia of religious hymns, Ourania of astronomy, Melpomene of tragedy Erato of erotic poetry, and Clio of history.

3) The three goddesses known as the Fates or Moirae (their ancient Greek name) were responsible for deciding the destinies of all humans. The ancient Greeks thought that the Fates were responsible for the intricate weaving of each person's life's thread. A person's life was a thread spun by Clotho, the goddess of creation, measured by Lachesis, who was the goddess of fate and cut by Atropos, who was the goddess of death. You may remember this idea from the Disney picture Hercules from 1997. In that telling, the Fates are confused with the Graeae, another group of three women in Greek mythology. The Graeae were crone-like figures who each had one eye and one tooth.

4) As was touched on briefly previously, the Furies, also known as the Erinyes (which was their original Greek name), were deities who represented wrath and punishment. These goddesses were in charge of meting out punishment to

mankind for their transgressions, notably the killing of members of their own families. Their names were Alecto, Megaera, and Tisiphone, and they were portrayed as hideous beings with wings, snakes for hair, or snakes curled around their limbs. They were given names in Greek mythology.

5) Monsters known as sirens were described as being half women and half birds. They were notorious for their song, which they used to seduce sailors into abandoning their ships and going to their doom. Despite their terrible appearance, they had stunning beauty. It was necessary to fill one's ears with wax to ensure that not even a single note of the sirens' song could enter one's hearing. This was the only method to successfully navigate past the sirens. It is well known that Odysseus wanted to hear the Sirens singing, so he tied himself to the mast of his ship to hear it without having to leap into the ocean (the sailors aboard his ship protected themselves with wax, they did not become sick.).

6) The most well-known creatures who were only partially human were called satyrs and centaurs. The upper half of a satyr's body was that of a human, while the bottom half was that of a goat, and they were known for making mischief (both humorous and serious!). The exception to this rule was Chiron, who was a wise mentor to many of the heroes and served as the model for the character of a satyr named

Phil in the animated film Hercules!, which was released in 1997. Other than Chiron, centaurs were monstrous creatures consisting of human heads and horse bodies.

Chapter 2 The Olympians

The pantheon of gods that were worshiped in ancient Greece is rather wide. You may find a god or a minor deity representing everything you can think of. What about dawn and dusk? Some gods can help with that. What about some epic poetry? There is a source of inspiration for that. Even smaller waterways, such as rivers and streams, probably had their deities dedicated to them. But the Olympian gods were the ones that mattered since they were the first gods, defeated the Titans and were responsible for creating the world as we know it. Zeus delegated many duties to the other Olympians, including creating Earth's flora, fauna, and even its inhabitants (humans).

The Olympians held the mistaken belief that since they were responsible for creating everything on Earth, including its inhabitants, they had the right to torment those same people. The Olympians were responsible for an infinite number of issues that the people of Earth experienced. Sometimes they would "fall in love" with the people of Earth, and other times they would bring storms and plagues upon them. Sometimes they would bring both. However, there was never any genuine love between them; rather, there was a craving for power and control. The Olympians sought a lot of power.

There had always been twelve Olympians, but the identities of those twelve changed depending on the era and the source of information. At various periods, they were composed of Zeus, Poseidon, and Hera, as well as Hades, Demeter, and Hestia. Hera was the mother of Zeus and Poseidon. Occasionally Demeter is an Olympian while Hades is not, and other times it's the other way around. Sometimes Demeter is an Olympian while Hades is not, and sometimes it's the other way around. As time went on and the mythology and legends of the gods continued to develop, Hestia, like the other Olympian gods, eventually lost her place at the table. From there, children of the earliest family members joined the group: the twin's Apollo and Artemis, Athena, and Hermes (all children of Zeus); child of Hera; Ares, Hephaestus, child of Zeus and Hera; sometimes the daughter of Zeus Aphrodite, sometimes the daughter of Ouranos (you can read all about it in Aphrodite's entry); and Dionysus, the last Olympian to join the fray, replacing Hestia. In Greek mythology, Dionysus was a one-of-a-kind figure since he was the offspring of Zeus and a regular human woman.

Chapter 3 Greek Gods

3.1 Zeus: God of the Sky

Zeus was considered to be the monarch of all the gods. Theoretically, he was the god of the sky, the weather, and other such things; nevertheless, in reality, he was the god of all gods; the deity who always had his way; the god who used his power and influence to bring about the demise of almost everyone he came into touch with. Although he is included in almost every popular cultural interpretation of Greek mythology, Zeus was nothing like the doting father portrayed by Disney in the film Hercules. Instead, Zeus was more like the version portrayed by Liam Neeson in the film Clash of the Titans (2010). Zeus used his time by setting gods against each other and descending on any and every woman (and occasionally males) he came across to "seduce" them or "carry them off." These ladies may be humans, nymphs, or goddesses. These phrases, like many others, are just euphemisms for what Zeus allegedly did to them, which was to attack them. There are endless instances of Zeus preying upon gods and humans who were unaware of what he was about to do to them.

Zeus was most famous for his thunderbolts, the weapons he used to defeat his foes and served as a symbol of his authority over the sky and the weather. In ancient times, eagles were associated with the god Zeus and were often seen as portending important events (in the Iliad, the story of the Trojan War, an eagle holding a snake in its talons was seen as a message from Zeus). Last but not least, the bull was often connected with Zeus because he chose to manifest himself as a bull, even if it was not always an express sign of Zeus (see the entry on Europa).

In Greek mythology, the King of the Gods was also the Father of several Mortals, considered the most important. Heracles was Zeus' son by a lady called Alcmene, while Perseus was Zeus' son by a woman named Dana. Both of these heroes were descended from Zeus. Minos, the great monarch of Crete and the purpose of the ancient Cretan civilization renowned as the Minoans, was the son of Zeus and a woman called Europa. Minos was the purpose of the historical Cretan culture known as the Minoans. Both the legendary Helen of Sparta (and subsequently, Troy) and her terrible sister Clytemnestra was (kind of, but we'll get to that later) Zeus' children by a lady called Leda. Helen was Zeus' daughter first, while Clytemnestra was Zeus' daughter second.

This does not mean an exhaustive list of Zeus's offspring; rather, it is only sampling some of the most well-known ones. For both literal and symbolic reasons, the monarch of the gods was sometimes referred to as the father of the gods. This was a title that he held. Although most of the gods you will learn about in this book have unique tales related to them directly, the tales involving Zeus include so many other gods and humans that those tales are presented in each of their entries.

3.2 Poseidon: God of the Sea

Poseidon was a legendary Olympian, a brother of Zeus, and the god of the sea. He was one of the original gods that the Olympians worshiped. Poseidon was also known as the god of horses, a belief that most likely originated from the observation that waves resemble running horses. The ancient Greeks had the belief that Poseidon was responsible for causing earthquakes, and as a result, they gave him the epithet "Earth-shaker." An epithet is similar to a nickname but is often used in combination with a person's given name. Both horses and dolphins were considered to be symbols of Poseidon. Additionally, Poseidon was often shown in artwork riding a chariot pushed by a hippocamp, a creature that was half horse and half fish.

Poseidon wed the nymph Amphitrite, and the couple went on to have several offspring together; among them, Triton was the most famous. In the animated picture "The Little Mermaid," released in 1989, this son of Poseidon serves as the inspiration for Ariel's father's name. Poseidon, rather than Poseidon's son, is the inspiration for the character of that Atlantican ruler in the movie. In "The Little Mermaid," Triton is shown as wielding a trident, much like Poseidon. In contrast to the portrayal of Triton in the movie, Poseidon did not have a reputation for being very kind or kind. Instead, he was famous for being... difficult and for the punishments, he meted out to heroes and mortals who did not expect them. Poseidon, like his brother Zeus, was notorious for his propensity to sexually abuse women and nymphs. In the Percy Jackson book series, Poseidon also played the role of Percy's (Perseus's) father (though, mythologically, Perseus was the son of Zeus, whereas Theseus was often described as the son of Poseidon).

According to legend, Poseidon (with Apollo) erected the walls around the famed city of Troy but subsequently sent a sea monster to destroy the city when its King didn't appropriately thank him for the walls! Even though the hero Heracles finally successfully killed the sea monster, thus rescuing the city of Troy, Poseidon would not let go of his resentment.

3.3 Hades: God of the Underworld and Wealth; God and King of the Dead

Hades, along with Zeus and Poseidon, was a member of the ancient pantheon of Olympian gods. He was the offspring of the titans Kronos and Rhea. You may recognize him as the villain with the flaming hair in Disney's Hercules or as the gorgeous love interest in Rachel Smythe's Lore Olympus (two very different versions of the deity!). He was also the inspiration for the god Hades in Greek mythology. Although he was known as the god of the dead and the underworld, Hades was not the deity of passing away (that was a guy named Thanatos). In addition to this, he was the deity of plenty and fortune. One of his Latin names, Dis, literally translates to "wealthy." During the conflict between the gods and the titans, Hades wore an invisibility helmet crafted by the Cyclops. Although this equipment seems awesome, it doesn't play a significant role in the mythology narrative.

Persephone, Hades's niece and the woman he had abducted when she was young, was Hades's wife (awkward). The beginnings of their narrative are terrible and horrific, yet, things do manage to turn out rather favorably for all involved people in the end (a real feat in Greek mythology). Even though he was the god of the dead and is often shown as the antagonist in works of popular culture, Hades was, other than the fact that he abducted Persephone, one of the Olympian gods who caused the least amount of trouble. Hades did not cheat on his wife, and it seemed they had come to love or, at the very least, respect one another. They appeared to enjoy a happy life together in the Underworld. Aside from that, he generally stayed to himself, recording the names of those who had passed away and causing other gods or living humans as little disruption as possible. Even though his brother Zeus was a far greater threat, hapless Hades is almost always portrayed as the antagonist.

Although "Hades" was the name of the deity who ruled the Underworld, the word may also be used to refer to the Underworld itself; for example, "Heracles journeyed to Hades to kidnap a dog" (for more information on Heracles's mad mission, see the next section on Cerberus). Tartarus is another name for the Underworld; however, this term may apply to a particular region of the Underworld or the Underworld as a whole. The Underworld is also sometimes referred to as Hades. The most common use of this term refers to the location of all the everlasting punishments carried out there.

3.4 Apollo: God of Music, Prophecy, Healing and Plague

He was also known as Phoebus Apollo, which derives from the fact that his grandmother, the Titan Phoebe, gave him the name Phoebus, which means "bright." Apollo was the god of music, prophecy, healing, and pestilence. Additionally, he was the identical brother of the goddess Artemis. Their mother was the Titan Leto, and the tale of how they came into the world is exciting. Apollo was one of the most influential and well-known deities in Greek mythology, even though he was not one of the original Olympians who triumphed over the Titans. He and his sister shared the responsibility of looking out for the welfare of youngsters. He was in charge of guarding the young men, while Artemis was in charge of the young women.

As the god of music, Apollo was connected with the nine Muses, and he was often shown holding the lyre, a traditional musical instrument in ancient Greece. Apollo's influence on the world was extensive. Since Apollo was also considered the deity of prophecy, the renowned Oracle of Delphi was said to have been named for him. It was often thought that Apollo might be heard speaking via the Pythia, the woman who served as the Oracle's intermediary. In actuality and fiction, the ancient Greeks would travel great distances to see the Oracle to consult with her and ask her inquiries. In mythology, the overarching theme of the Oracle's prophesies was that humanity would struggle to escape the doom that the Oracle predicted, but in doing so, they would unintentionally bring about the fate that the Oracle had predicted. Apollo, the god of healing (as well as equally the deity of plague and disease), was in charge of medicine, which he conferred to the lesser god Asclepius, the god of medicine, and his daughter Hygieia. Apollo was also the god of plague and illness (the goddess of cleanliness and hygiene).

Apollo eventually got confused with the Titan Helios, who was the deity of the sun in later versions of Greek mythology. Because of this, even in modern times, he is often shown as the driver of the chariot that drove the sun across the sky daily. In the beginning, this responsibility belonged to Helios, but as time passed, the number of mythological figures diminished, and Apollo found himself in a position to assume it.

3.5 Hephaestus: God of Fire, Craftsmanship, and Sculpture

Hephaestus was the Greek deity of fire, blacksmithing, sculpting, and other forms of workmanship. He was a member of the Olympian race and conceived by the goddess Hera all alone. Hera was infuriated with her husband, Zeus, since he continually cheated on her with other women, nymphs, and goddesses and, through those women, generated an increasing number of offspring who were not her own! Hera often thought that Zeus's exploits were being held up as an example for everyone to see. Specifically, Hera believed that Zeus had shown that he did not need the company of women at all under the birth of his daughter Athena. In actual honesty, Metis was Athena's mother; yet, when Zeus "gave birth" to her himself (even if her bursting out of his brain isn't precisely the same thing as "giving birth"), he was showing off. Hera gave birth to Hephaestus all by herself to exact revenge on Zeus and demonstrate that she was as competent as he was.

Hephaestus was not thought to be one of the more handsome or alluring gods; in fact, the reverse was true of him. This was a source of ongoing aggravation for Hephaestus's wife, Aphrodite. Hephaestus, on the other hand, is represented in Disney's Hercules (the 1998 TV series) as a stocky, muscular deity, but Ares, who Aphrodite did find quite lovely, is shown as quite the opposite.

In the myths surrounding Hephaestus, he is often shown as concocting various schemes and devices to deceive and catch gods and goddesses who have offended him in some manner.

3.6 Ares: God of War, Courage, and Civil Order

Ares, the Greek god of war, was famous for stirring up the combatants on both sides of the conflict. Even though he was a significant deity, many tales do not mention Ares. His primary relationship is with Aphrodite, the goddess he loved but was forced to give up when she married Hephaestus. Together, they were responsible for the birth of many offspring, including the goddess of harmony known as Harmonia, the personifications of horror and dread known as Phobos and Deimos, and (according to some traditions) Eros, the god of love and sexual desire.

Ares was always depicted with his warrior's helmet, either wearing it or holding it, and he frequently appears in pop culture representations of Greek mythology. He is the main antagonist in the film Wonder Woman (2017), and he also appears in the films Wrath of the Titans (2012) and Immortals (2017). Ares was always shown with the helmet, either wearing it or holding it (2011). In addition, he plays a significant role in the first book of the Percy Jackson series. Ares, like Hades, is often represented as a villain in popular culture, even though in mythology, he was seldom, if ever, the antagonist. One of the more realistic depictions of Ares in popular culture can be found in the game Lore Olympus. Ares is a god of battle, but that doesn't automatically make him a villain.

Ares had a strong relationship with the goddess Eris, known in Roman and Latin as Discordia. Eris was the goddess of conflict and discord. Eris gained notoriety not just for her part in igniting the Trojan War (for more information on this, see Paris's section) but also for her penchant for wreaking havoc on battlefields and calling for more deaths. They often traveled during the Trojan War on the same horse, even though Eris's passion for bloodshed outshone even that of Ares.

3.7 Hermes: God of Herds and Flocks, Travelers, Trade, Writing, Athleticism, and Astronomy; the Messenger God

In addition to his role as the second messenger for the Olympian gods, Hermes was a deity of many other things (the other was a goddess named Iris). For instance, he assumed the persona of the "trickster deity," a character that often appears in ancient tales. Hermes was born to Zeus and the Pleiadean nymph Maia, who were the parents of the Pleiades (sisters who were eventually placed in the sky as the constellation with the same name). You undoubtedly remember him from Disney's

Hercules, in which he played the role of Hercules' hip, quick-witted sidekick and Zeus' messenger. He wore sunglasses and wore them constantly.

Hermes was given the name Argeiphontes, which translates to "Slayer of Argus," when he murdered the gigantic Argus Panoptes, who Hera cherished. Hermes did this in an attempt to rescue the Naiad Io.

3.8 Dionysus: God of Theater, Wine, Vegetation, Pleasure, and Madness

Dionysus was known as the deity of festivity and celebration. He was the god of many things, but the ones that were most essential to him were wine, pleasure, and the theater. The only Olympian to be born to a human mother, Semele gave birth to Dionysus. Because of this, he is a descendent of Cadmus, the man who founded Thebes. Because of this, he was connected to the history of that city and the family curse, even though it did not affect him. At the same time, Dionysus was often portrayed as a deity who had traveled from Asia to the ancient Greek civilization. Even yet, there is evidence that Dionysus was one of the first gods worshipped in the Greek world, appearing in texts from the oldest languages spoken by the Greeks. These inscriptions date back to the Bronze Age. As the Roman deity Liber, Dionysus was adored for a time that exceeded that of most of the other Olympian gods. He was also the god who was revered for the longest. Dionysus was often shown in art as a youthful gender-fluid figure holding a glass for drinking wine and his thyrsus, a reed staff.

There is enough information about Dionysus to fill several volumes, even though his worship was somewhat variable. To put it another way, he was a god of the people, a deity with whom common people on earth could connect more than they could with any other Olympians. This was shown by the fact that his emblems were alcohol and stage performances.

Since Dionysus was the theater god, the plays performed in ancient Greece were all about him. The Dionysia was the most important event for the performance of ancient Greek plays. It was an annual festival in Athens and included a competition between three writers for the highest award. It would always start with a sacrifice to Dionysus and involve a parade of phyllo (yep, sculptures of male genitalia) traversing the city.

Chapter 4 Greek Goddess

4.1 Hestia: Goddess of the Hearth and Home

Hestia was a goddess in ancient Greece who was revered as one of the most significant goddesses in everyday life. She was a virgin. She was worshipped daily due to her status as the goddess of the hearth and home. She was believed responsible for domestic life and, therefore, domestic bliss. In this capacity, she was entitled to a share of the offerings presented to the gods. Hestia would preside over the feast prepared using the leftover piece of the animal that was offered as a sacrifice to the gods by the ancient Greeks after they had slaughtered the animal. In addition, every ancient city and town would have a public hearth dedicated to Hestia, and the fire that was kept burning there was never allowed to go out.

Hestia was both the eldest and youngest of the Olympians. Since she was the firstborn child of Kronos and Rhea, she was also the first Olympian to be consumed by Kronos. Because of this, she was the one he regurgitated very last after his defeat at the hands of Zeus. Because of this, Hestia and Zeus were both the youngest children in their families.

Hestia managed to keep herself apart from the everyday drama that the other gods consumed. She kept her distance from both humanity and other gods, refusing to interact with either. There was a short period when Apollo and Poseidon were both interested in marrying Hestia; however, she made it very plain to both of them, as well as to Zeus, that she would not be marrying anybody and that she would keep her virginity until the end of her life. Hestia was only occasionally regarded as one of the Olympian gods, even though she maintained significance in the Greeks' lives, and the most probable explanation for this was a total indifference to the other gods who made up the Olympian pantheon.

The Romans ultimately adopted the religion of worshiping Hestia, which the Greeks had practiced. Her name in Roman and Latin was Vesta, and the Romans had a group of females who were dedicated to Vesta and kept the holy fire blazing in her temples. This group of girls was called the Vestal Virgins, and they were specifically chosen. These young women would become some of the most influential priestesses in Roman history.

4.2 Persephone: Goddess of Vegetation, Spring and the underworld

Persephone was the daughter of the goddess Demeter and the deity Zeus. She was the original goddess of springtime and development. The Greek names Kore and Persephone were used for Persephone before and after Hades abducted her, respectively. Kore was her name before Hades took her. In the beginning, they called her Kore, which has the meaning of "young girl" or "maiden" (as in "virgin"). After she was abducted, she changed her name to Persephone, which means "to destroy" or "to bring death" (which is a much more awesome translation), reflecting her new role as an infernal goddess of death and ruler of the Underworld. Persephone eventually established herself as the legitimate monarch of the underworld, despite the sad and troublesome circumstances surrounding her original descent into the underworld (for more on this, read the next narrative). Persephone continued to serve as the goddess of spring, but she also enthusiastically assumed the role of the infernal goddess of death. As a result, she became known as the Dread Goddess and was frequently held in higher esteem and dreaded more than her husband, who was the original god of the dead.

On Earth, Persephone shared time with her mother, Demeter, for part of the year, while she and her husband spent the other portion of the year in the underworld. When Persephone was with Demeter, the soil flourished, and every plant developed to its full potential. During her time with her husband, the crops wilted and were eventually buried by frost. As a result, she came to be connected not only with spring and the development process but also with the soil going into a state of dormancy throughout the winter months.

4.3 Hecate: Goddess of Magic, witchcraft, Ghosts, and Necromancy

Hecate is often considered one of the most enigmatic figures in Greek mythology. She was often shown in Greek art as carrying torches, and it is believed that she was the daughter of the Titans Perses and Asteria. In light of this, as well as the overall air of secrecy that surrounded her, some people believed that she was either a Titan herself or a minor deity; in any case; however, she was a fascinating, significant, and very potent witch. Hecate was skilled in the ancient Greek discipline of pharmacy, which included using various plants and herbs to produce medicinal concoctions (where we get the word pharmacy). It was claimed that Hecate had uncovered many toxic plants and concoctions, which she would use to adorn the tips of javelins and spears, making them much deadlier. Some accounts claim that Hecate would also put her concoctions and poisons to the test on random people she came into contact with. According to these accounts, she would give strangers poisoned food and observe their responses.

Hecate was most famous for assisting the goddess Demeter in locating her abducted daughter Persephone using the candles discussed before. Hecate was the one who overheard Persephone screaming, but she did not instantly understand who had abducted her daughter. After discovering that

Persephone was living with Hades in the Underworld, Hecate became her companion there in the kingdom of the dead.

It was thought that the witch goddess spent her time near crossroads or graves and that she was often followed by a polecat and a dog, the latter of which was previously a lady called Hecuba who reigned as queen of Troy. Hecuba was unwilling to serve as a slave for the Greeks following the fall of Troy; as a result, she leaped into the water, where she was later turned into a dog.

Hecate, along with several other goddesses from Greek mythology (like Hestia, for example), had a position of great significance in the ancient Greek world; nonetheless, there are very few tales, if any at all, that is documented about her.

4.4 Cerberus: Guardian of the underworld

Cerberus was Hades' trusted servant and watched over the underworld as Cerberus. Cerberus, a huge dog with three heads, was one of the most well-known "monsters" in Greek mythology. He was responsible for protecting the Underworld from uninvited visitors and ensuring that the souls of the deceased remained inside its confines. Cerberus is sometimes shown as having a snake for a tail and a mane made of snakes. This is even though he is most known for having the appearance of a dog with three heads. Some people believe that his saliva was toxic and that it was maybe used by the witch Hecate. Cerberus was a child of the primal monsters Typhon and Echidna, making him a brother to a number of the other monsters in mythology that are considered to be among the most formidable and well-known.

Within the canon of popular culture, a representation of Cerberus may be found in the first Harry Potter novel in the form of Hagrid's dog Fluffy, tasked with guarding the location of the philosopher's stone. In Greek mythology, he is most known for being caught by the hero Heracles as the twelfth and last task in the series of twelve labors that he must complete.

Heracles was tasked with traveling to the underworld, capturing the terrible Hound of Hades, Cerberus, and bringing him back with him. This task was given to Heracles by a character called Eurystheus. Eurystheus planned this to be how Heracles would be killed; he had no interest in seeing the monster dog. Some people believe that Heracles could finish the work with the assistance of Persephone. She is said to have given Heracles the dog, and he successfully returned the dog to Eurystheus. Others claim that Hades gave Heracles the dog with the condition that he had to prove that he could defeat the monster without using any weapons—in other words, he could only fight with his bare hands. Heracles was the most powerful of all the Greek heroes, and as a result, he was the one who could subdue Cerberus and bring him back to Eurystheus without any difficulty.

On his voyage to the underworld to retrieve his bride Eurydice, the legendary singer and hero Orpheus met with the three-headed dog Cerberus. Orpheus put the giant dog to sleep with music, much as he did with Fluffy in the Harry Potter books and movies.

4.5 Demeter: Goddess of Agriculture and the Harvest

As the daughter of Kronos and Rhea, Demeter was one of the firstborn gods. However, she is most well-known for being the mother of Persephone, who reigns as queen of the underworld. She was the goddess of agriculture and the harvest in ancient Greece; therefore, she regulated agricultural activities and had an important role in the ancient Greeks' day-to-day lives.

Demeter also became the presiding goddess of the Eleusinian Mysteries, which were the secret rituals of a "mystery cult." It was believed that initiates of the Eleusinian Mysteries would find themselves in a special place in the Underworld when they passed away, and that place was the blessed Elysium. These weren't like today's cults; rather, they were just groups of individuals whose worship and activities were kept a secret from anybody who wasn't formally inducted into the organization. The Eleusinian Mysteries were considered to be the pinnacle of all mystery cults that existed in ancient Greece.

The abduction of Demeter and Hades' daughter, Persephone, caused Demeter to experience a state of terror. At first, she was clueless about what had transpired concerning her daughter. During the nine days that Demeter spent searching the ground day and night for her daughter, she did not eat or drink anything since she was so focused on her mission. She eventually came face to face with the goddess of witchcraft, Hecate, who revealed to her that she had heard Persephone screaming when she was being abducted but had not seen who had stolen her. She extended an offer to assist Demeter in continuing her hunt. Together, they traveled to the home of the Titan Helios; being the deity responsible for the sun's movement across the sky daily, he would have seen the abduction of Persephone. Helios was the one who informed Demeter that Hades, the god of the underworld, had taken her daughter away from her. Helios also informed Demeter that the action had been carried out with the approval of Zeus.

The gods have a variety of peculiar methods at their disposal for granting immortality or invulnerability to humanity. Demeter and Thetis, Achilles' goddess mother, were responsible for the sacrifice of Demophoon. Demeter cast Demophoon into the flames of a raging fire while Thetis submerged Achilles in a boiling pot. Both ladies were discovered by inquisitive mortals who could not comprehend what they were doing, and as a result, the processes were halted (Peleus, Achilles's father, caught Thetis in the act), which ultimately had an impact on the outcomes of their offspring.

4.6 Hera: Goddess of Marriage, Woman, and Fertility; Queen of the Gods

In a twist of fate, Zeus wed Hera, the goddess of wedlock, and they had three children together (though Zeus was not particularly respectful of marital vows, she was). She was the goddess of marriage, but she was also the goddess who regularly punished women for their husbands' desires to have sex with them or attack them. Her husbands wanted to have sexual relations with them or assault them. Hera seldom punished Zeus himself, which may have been because it was far more difficult to punish the ruler of the gods than it was to punish human women or because she truly blamed the women. Either way, it is possible that Hera placed the responsibility on the women. Despite this, Hera's involvement in the majority of myths includes her attempting to have Zeus bring harm to women or the offspring of women.

Ares, the god of war, was their only Olympian child. Hebe, the goddess of youth (who eventually married Heracles), and Eileithyia, the goddess of childbirth, were all born to Zeus' wife, but the vast majority of Zeus' many, many children were born to other women. Zeus' wife was the mother of at least three of Zeus' children: Ares, the god of war, was also their only Olympian child. Hephaestus was Hera's second kid, whom she gave birth to alone without the assistance of Zeus or any other male. Hera was so enraged at her husband for continually cheating on her with other women (both with and without the agreement of those ladies), and she was even more enraged by the fact that those women were continually bringing him children (both gods and mortals). She was most angry with Athena, whom she saw as being born of Zeus alone (Athena did have a mother, but Zeus had eaten her! —see Athena's entry), and as a result, Hera impregnated herself with the god Hephaestus (his entry tells the full story), so that she could have a child who was all her own. Athena did have a mother, but Zeus had eaten her! —see Athena's entry

Hera was so traumatized by the fact that her cherished guardian, Argus Panoptes, was killed by Hermes (for more information on this story, see Io's entry) that she chose the peacock as her totem animal and memorialized the hundred-eyed giant by embedding each of his eyes in a feather of the peacock. According to a theory put out by the ancient Greeks, this is the reason peacocks have feathers that resemble eyes.

4.7 Athena: Goddess of Strategic War and Wisdom

Athena was the daughter Zeus held in the highest regard, and he made sure that everyone knew it throughout his whole life. She was the princess of the gods and the Titan Metis's daughter. Her father was Zeus, the ruler of the gods. Metis is said to have been Zeus' first wife, although some believe she was his first fling. In either scenario, Metis got pregnant with the goddess Athena when she and Zeus were together, and Athena was Zeus's daughter. However, not long after this event, Zeus found out that any kid of Metis was destined to be far smarter than he was. Zeus saw this possibility as an imminent danger and promptly set out to eradicate the possibility of any child being born to Metis. His answer to this so-called challenge was to ingest Metis as its whole.

However, even after Zeus had consumed Metis, she continued to carry Zeus' child from inside her tummy. After some time had passed, Zeus started to feel the effects of Metis's growing pregnancy inside of him. He suffered from a terrible headache, and the agony was so intense that he could not function normally. He discussed his situation with others who lived on Mount Olympus to get advice on how to deal with what he was going through. It was recommended that Zeus use an axe to hack at his skull since this would undoubtedly release the pressure and end his excruciating migraine. This was a good idea, so Zeus gave it his blessing and requested the deity Hephaestus to aim the axe. Hephaestus accomplished this, and out of the hole that he had just cut in Zeus's brain emerged Zeus's daughter Athena, fully grown and decked in armor with her shield in her hand.

One of the most well-known deities is named Athena. She was revered as the protector deity of several important ancient towns, one of which was Athens. Minerva, derived from the Roman goddess of wisdom and courage, was chosen to be Professor McGonagall's first name in the Harry Potter books. This choice was most likely made to convey the qualities of McGonagall.

It was believed that the myth of Athena and Arachne explained how the first spiders came into being on Earth. Spiders are creatures that spin complex webs that are vulnerable to being destroyed. The term "arachnid" originates from the ancient Greek word "arachne," which translates to "spider."

4.8 Aphrodite: Goddess of Love, Beauty, and Sex

Everyone is familiar with Aphrodite, the Greek goddess of love, since she is one of the most well-known Greek gods, along with Athena. Aphrodite was famed for both her stunning appearance (which she was well aware of) and her ability to arouse a desire to engage in sexual activity. She was identified with the island of Cyprus and was often referred to as the Cyprian Goddess. She was born off the coast of Cyprus. Others assert that she was the offspring of Zeus and the Titan Dione, even though others believe she was created from the foam produced when Ouranos was castrated.

Although Aphrodite and the deity Hephaestus were legally married, theirs was not pleasant. When Zeus sought to liberate Hera from Hephaestus's trap, she was married off to Hephaestus, which was very much against her will (see Hephaestus's page for more information). Aphrodite had extramarital relationships with several gods when she married Hephaestus, including Ares, Adonis, Hermes, Dionysus, and Poseidon. She and Ares were the parents of several children, including the goddess Harmonia and, according to some accounts, Eros, the god of love and sexual desire. Other offspring were born to the couple as well. She and Ares were infamously caught in a very sticky circumstance, which served as an example of one of the many nights they spent together.

Hermaphroditus was the name of the kid that the goddess Aphrodite and the deity Hermes had together. This child's name was a portmanteau of the names of both of his parents. Hermaphroditus had a chance to meet with a nymph named Salmacis when he was an adult, and the two of them eventually combined into a single being. They evolved into the world's first known intersex persons, according to Greek mythology.

4.9 Artemis: Goddess of the Hunt and Wilderness

Artemis, the goddess of the hunt and the wild, was the identical twin sister of the deity Apollo. Artemis was revered as the protector of the forest. Leto gave birth to Artemis when she had finally located a location where it was safe for her to give birth (for further background information, see the section for Leto). After Leto gave birth to Artemis, the newly born goddess assisted her mother through the delivery of her twin brother, Apollo. As a result of this act, Artemis came to be identified with the process of giving birth. In addition to her other roles, the goddess watched over and protected young women, just as her brother did for young men.

Artemis was famed as a virgin goddess who refused to have any contact or attention from males. Even the priestesses who served in the temples dedicated to Artemis were required to keep their virginity, just like the goddess herself. It was common knowledge that she spent her time with a group of nymphs. Together, they would hunt and explore the woods, take a dip in the rivers and lakes, and enjoy themselves in the great outdoors. The bow and arrows were Artemis's go-to weapon of choice, and she was an absolute pro at using them. She wore a short dress, held her bow and arrow, and sometimes even had an animal pelt thrown over her shoulder. Artemis was generally shown in a hunting outfit. She often traveled through the woods with her nymph entourage while riding in a chariot dragged through the undergrowth by deer.

Before Artemis would allow the Greeks to fight in the Trojan War, she demanded that they perform a human sacrifice in her honor. This was quite out of character for the goddess Artemis. Agamemnon, the leader of the Greeks as they prepared to go to war, had irritated Artemis. To appease her, he offered his daughter Iphigenia in what is believed to be one of the few instances of a human sacrifice to the gods. Iphigenia was thrown into the sea.

The bear and the stag, which are Artemis's holy creatures, each stand in for a different mortal being whom the goddess Artemis has wronged in some manner. The bear, of course, originates from Callisto, whose unfortunate ending Artemis felt responsible for, and the stag originates from Actaeon, who was a hunter (whose story is told in his entry).

Chapter 5 Deities

In Greek mythology, there are many different kinds of humanoid creatures that make up the pantheon. In this part, we will discuss the characters with varied degrees of divinity. These are people who are not only humans or even heroes, but they are also not considered to be among the primary gods who rule Mount Olympus. These are the tales of titans, nymphs, minor gods, monsters, and the gods themselves.

The Olympian gods covered in Part 2 appear in most of the tales covered in this area as well; nonetheless, it is the non-Olympian deities, whether they be benevolent, evil, or monstrous, who are the most prominent characters in this section. The dramatic and tragic lives of other heavenly beings are the focus of these characters' backstories, which, although still significant and famous, are less centered on the Olympians and more on the lives of other divine creatures. There is the Titan who tried to give human civilization fire and was condemned for it; there is the Titan-mother of the Olympian twins, sought by a vengeance deity; there is a nymph destroyed by a god but able to make a beautiful thing as a consequence; there is the god of love who fell in love; there is the beginning of echoes and narcissists; and there are the gigantic parents of all of the most exciting creatures from Greek mythology Some of the most famous, significant, and well-known tales from Greek mythology are those that pertain to non-Olympian deities. This phrase is used here in a wide sense to refer to persons who are divine in some manner and who are not human. The creatures and their similarly horrific offspring are eerie and interesting, which is an added benefit.

5.1 Prometheus: A Titan; God of Forethought

Prometheus and his brother Epimetheus, known as the god of an afterthought, were among the Titans that fought on the side of the Olympian gods during the Titanomachy, a conflict that saw numerous titans pitted against one other. Not only is Prometheus renowned for giving humanity fire, but he is also famous for fooling Zeus into letting people keep the finest slices of sacrifice meat for themselves. This is another reason why Prometheus is so well-known. He was the deity of planning and being prepared. In his family, Prometheus was known as the forward thinker since he was the one who always gave careful consideration to his deeds before carrying them out. (His brother was the complete antithesis of him.)

The gods charged Prometheus and Epimetheus with the responsibility of bringing mankind into being, as recounted in certain versions of the myth of humanity's birth. But since Epimetheus was not particularly skilled in these areas, he gave all the significant characteristics to the animals and did not save any for humans (hair, scales, and camouflage were all taken!). As a result, humans do not possess any of these characteristics today. Because Prometheus felt sorry for the newly created humans and the fact that they were defenseless, he decided to bestow upon them the capacity to walk upright and the power to make fire. These were the only two things he could conceive that would give mankind an advantage over animals.

Circe, the protagonist of Madeline Miller's story, comes upon Prometheus as he is serving his sentence, which is to be chained to a rock. Circe then kills Prometheus. Because of her time with him, she develops an understanding for others that can only come from knowing Prometheus.

5.2 Pandora: The First Woman

According to Greek mythology, Pandora was the first woman to ever live on this planet. She was presented to the men who were already there as both a blessing and a burden in the form of a gift. There are two distinct retellings of the myth of Pandora, and each is interesting in its own right. The first one is a continuation of the tale that began with Prometheus: Zeus was upset with the Titan because he had given the humans, who at the time comprised solely of males, the fire that had been stolen from Mount Olympus as well as the best portions of meat when they were offering a sacrifice. He intended to exact revenge not just on humanity but also on Prometheus. His retribution for the human race consisted of the production of females (a tired and very offensive stereotype!). Clay was used by Zeus's son

Hephaestus to fashion the first woman, who Zeus then had Hephaestus bring to life. Pandora, the first lady, was stunning, brilliant, and lovely in her appearance. Zeus arranged for the other gods to bestow on her talents and flaws, such as Athena teaching her how to weave, Aphrodite making her elegant, and Hermes giving her a cunning nature. According to this interpretation of the legend, she was not only cunning but also fundamentally wicked, and as a result, all the women who were her descendants had this trait. This is not the most sympathetic tale, nor does it provide an explanation for any of the lovely ladies in Greek mythology (not to mention the fact that it is sexist).

The second tale of Pandora is not quite as sexist as the first when it comes to all women. It starts the same way the other one did, with Zeus desiring to punish Prometheus for stealing fire from the Olympians and Hephaestus being tasked with creating Pandora by Zeus. Pandora was given a jar, more generally known as a box, and explicit instruction not to open it. In this version of the story, Pandora is not the personification of all evil; consequently, neither are all women. She was then transported to the Titan Epimetheus and given to him as a new bride. The instruction that Epimetheus should not take any presents from the gods was given to him by his brother Prometheus, but, as Epimetheus was the god of an afterthought, he swiftly forgot this advise and accepted the gifts nonetheless.

Soon after their wedding, Epimetheus and Pandora were joined in matrimony, and shortly afterward, Pandora began to wonder what was contained in the jar that had been bestowed to her by the gods. She had an inquisitive nature, a trait shared by many smart individuals, and she wanted to find out what was within. She broke the seal on the jar, and the contents spilled out into the world, bringing with them all the worst horrors, diseases, and evils. As soon as she realized what she'd done, she slammed the lid on the jar as fast as possible. The only thing left inside was hope, humanity's sole line of defense and source of solace against the challenges of the outside world.

In this telling of the tale, women are not innately bad; they are so naturally curious that they unintentionally bring all of the world's ills onto themselves and their offspring. Neither of these tales is very respectful toward women, but they both provide light on the ancient Greeks' attitudes toward women in general and are thus instructive. Pandora is also connected with hope, and the significance of hope in the lives of mankind is underlined to a significant degree throughout the story.

5.3 Leto: A Titan; Goddess of Motherhood; Protector of the Young

Leto was a Titan and the goddess of maternity. She was also known as the Titaness. Leto was a guardian of the young in addition to the roles that Artemis and Apollo played in her life. She was the mother of two of the most significant gods in Greek mythology and the daughter of Coeus, the god of logical intelligence, and Phoebe, the goddess of brilliant, sparkling intellect. She was a daughter of the Titans Coeus and Phoebe (though Apollo far outweighed his sister in that respect). Phoebe was known for her oracular and prophetic mind, but Coeus's brain was considered more grounded in reality. It is not apparent what made Phoebe's intellect so brilliant and sparkling.

At the beginning of the legend of the Titans, gods, and Olympians, Zeus and Leto married one another. It is unknown if this was a relationship based on love and affection or whether it was one of the countless assaults perpetrated by Zeus, but regardless, Leto fell pregnant with twins at this time. As time passed, Hera learned the truth about Zeus and Leto, including that Leto was pregnant, and she was enraged. Hera swore solemnly that she would do all in her power to stop Leto from giving birth. Hera could be utterly scary when she wanted to be (and she often wanted to be when punishing women Zeus associated himself with), and as a result, nobody wanted to make her angry since she could be so terrible when she did want to be.

Leto walked about aimlessly, looking for a birthing facility when she was pregnant. She made her way across Greece and Asia Minor, but no one was willing to help her. This may have been the result of people's concern that allowing Leto to give birth in their region would lead Hera to get enraged, or it may have been a more specific, magical method of keeping Leto from giving birth physically. Either explanation is possible. Leto did not stop looking until she saw what seemed to be a floating island (it was believed that this island was not attached to the earth; instead, it floated through the sea, unmoored). Because the island was not connected to the rest of the world in the same way that the other places Leto had visited were, she was able to give birth there. The wrath of Hera did not affect it.

Leto was responsible for giving birth to the goddess Artemis first, and Artemis later assisted her mother in the delivery of Apollo, the second of Leto's twin children. As a result, Artemis is known as the goddess of pregnancy and childbirth. From the moment Apollo was born there, the island became holy to him. It was given the name Delos (this island is very significant in the history of ancient Greece, and it was holy even before it was ascribed as the birthplace of the twins), and it was given this name because of its location. As a unit, the family of three gods served as guardians over the younger generations.

Asteria, Leto's sister and a Titan, is known for her role as the parent of Hecate, the goddess of witchcraft, via her union with the Titan Perses. Asteria was another one of Zeus's targets (the list is limitless!), but she could evade him after changing herself into a quail and running away. According to another version of the story, Leto arrived on the island of Delos because Asteria, after transforming herself into a quail, dove into the water to further elude Zeus. Her transformation into the island, known as Delos when Apollo was born there, took place while she was still submerged in the ocean.

5.4 Daphne: A Nymph

Apollo, the god of music and poetry, became enamored with the Naiad nymph Daphne, who presided over freshwater springs. She had the same role as Artemis, that of a huntress. She didn't care what guys thought of her and had a passion for wild adventures in the woods. Bernini's sculpture of Apollo and Daphne is perhaps the most well-known and stunning representation of her; it is also one of the most common. In the Disney film Hercules, an unidentified nymph, runs away from Hercules's companion and trainer, Phil, by transforming herself into a tree. Even though the heroine in the film is not called Daphne, this sequence is based on her life and the events she went through.

Daphne was often portrayed as Apollo's spouse throughout Greek mythology. Because he loved her so much, most people did not see their history as especially troublesome. It was perceived as a lovely narrative in which Apollo received his holy tree rather than a story in which a woman was forced to convert herself into an item to escape from a man's hands. This was because women were considered to be the property of males at the time.

5.5 Eros: God of Erotic Love and Sex

Eros was the son of Aphrodite and Ares, a couple who were never legally united but who spawned some of the most notable offspring of Greek mythology. Alternatively, he is often characterized as a kid of simply Chaos itself! While his mother, Aphrodite, was revered as the goddess of love in general, Eros was known as the god of sexually explicit love. Although this figure became linked more with childish cherubs than the adult man of Greek mythology, Eros was maybe better recognized by his Roman name, Cupid.

Eros was famed for his bow and arrows, either tipped with a very powerful love potion or an equally powerful potion that persuaded its victims that they utterly detested the first person they saw. Both potions were on the end of the arrows he shot. Eros had tremendous power because of these instruments, albeit he utilized them for humorous effect most of the time.

Even though this tale is told solely in a Roman piece of literature called Apuleius's The Golden Ass, it is Eros's love for a lady named Psyche that is the most well-known aspect of his character (also known as Metamorphoses). Their tale is one of a kind; it is not often that a myth is told in just one place and goes on to achieve the kind of notoriety that this one achieved.

Because a Roman narrated their tale, the gods are referred to by their Roman names in the entry after this one.

5.6 Psyche: A Princess; Later, the Goddess of the Soul

Apelleius, who was Psyche's storyteller, didn't trouble himself with specifying which country Psyche belonged to or what her title was. The essential quality of Psyche, as depicted in the myth, was her stunning good looks, which attracted admirers from around the ancient world. As soon as she wed Cupid, she was elevated to the status of a goddess and took on the job of the goddess of the soul (the psyche).

In artwork, she is often shown as having butterfly wings, unlike Cupid, who has angel wings. The sculpture Psyche Revived by Cupid's Kiss, created by Antonio Canova and comes in two different iterations, is often regarded as the best artistic representation of Cupid and Psyche. In the version that is kept in the Louvre in Paris, Psyche does not have any wings. On the other hand, the version kept in the Metropolitan Museum of Art in New York City has Psyche with butterfly wings. In the webcomic, Lore Olympus, the tale of Cupid and Psyche is featured prominently as part of an ongoing plotline. It is also recounted in the book Till We Have Faces, which C.S. Lewis wrote.

The tale of Psyche prevailing over Venus's ordeals is a parable about the resilience of the human spirit and the capacity of people to triumph over adversity and make up for past transgressions. It's also one of the few examples of a genuine love tale with a happy ending.

5.7 Echo and Narcissus: A Nymph and a Young Mortal Man (the Son of a River God and a Nymph)

Echo was an Oread, a mountain nymph, and she liked socializing with other nymphs on Mount Cithaeron, located in Boeotia. On the other hand, these nymphs cared more about Zeus than Artemis. Although he was the offspring of a river deity and a nymph, Narcissus did not seem to have inherited any of his parents' divine characteristics, despite being a beautiful young man. Even though their history is sadder than romantic, the couple is often represented in many art forms.

Echo was thought to be the source of echoes by the ancient Greeks, which is not unexpected given their culture. Hers is the sole voice that can be heard echoing through tunnels across the planet, and it can only repeat the most recent phrase said by anybody close. Also, the term "narcissism" and its philosophy come from Narcissus, as does the flower that bears his name, the narcissus. This shouldn't come as much of a surprise, either.

5.8 Typhon and Echidna

Typhon and Echidna were considered to be among the very first monsters described in Greek mythology. Both Typhon and Echidna were born of Gaia and Tartarus, but Ceto, a notorious sea monster, gave birth to Echidna. Phorcys gave birth to Typhon (a primordial sea god). Together, Typhon and Echidna were responsible for the birth of the most infamous monsters in mythology.

- There are various ways to characterize Typhon, including the following: Sometimes he takes the form of a storm monster, but most of the time, he takes on a serpentine appearance. The bottom half of his body consisted of two snake tails, while the upper half was that of a man. This is a frequent description of him. And to ensure he didn't appear too natural, each of his fingers was wrapped with a hundred snakes. There is a common misconception that Typhon has wings. She had the upper half of a lady, and her bottom half was a coiled snake. Echidna's description is similar, except it is less horrifying:

- The following are examples of Typhon and Echidna's hideous descendants:

- The three-headed dog, Cerberus, served as a guardian at the gateway to the underworld.

- The multi-headed Hydra may be found in Heracles' entry.

- The Chimera was a mythical creature that resembled a lion but could breathe fire, had the head of a goat sticking out of its back, and had a snake for a tail (the Chimera was killed by the hero Bellerophon with the help of the famous flying horse Pegasus).

- The Crommyonian Sow was a dragon-like pig that breathed fire and was ultimately slain by Theseus.

- The Caucasian Eagle, also known as the eagle, that Zeus sent to Prometheus to devour his liver indefinitely.

- The Hesperian Dragon was a legendary creature that was said to have served as a guardian for the Garden of the Hesperides.

- The Sphinx was an entity with the characteristics of a woman, a lion, and an eagle (for further information, check the section on Oedipus).

- The Lion of Nemea.

They had a lot of children!

Some accounts dispute the idea that Typhon spent eternity in Tartarus. The legend has it that Typhon was imprisoned under the Italian island of Sicily and that the ongoing volcanic activity of today's Mount Etna is proof of his ongoing wrath there.

In one telling of the conflict between Zeus and Typhon, Typhon succeeds in ripping all of Zeus' muscles off his body. The Marriage of Cadmus and Harmony, a book by Roberto Calasso, is a stunning retelling of Greek tales in which the hero Cadmus restores Zeus's sinews to his body.

Chapter 6 Heroes and Mortals

Whether they were heroes or not, Mortals in Greek mythology played an important part in how the ancient Greeks interpreted the natural world and the workings of the gods. This includes both heroes and non-heroes. Although this is not the case in every tale, many tales that center on humans serve as illustrations of how the gods interacted with human life, whether for the better or for, the worse (it was usually worse).

A significant number of the tales in this section concern women who met their ends at the hands of Zeus for one reason or another. Even though the ancient Greeks adored and revered Zeus, they knew that he and the other gods could do terrible acts for very little or no apparent cause. This portrayal was their method of comprehending how someone from the human race might accomplish the same thing. Several tales discuss the hubris of mortals or those who felt they were just as competent or even more capable than the gods (these comparisons never went well for the humans). And then there are the heroes, who are (mostly) males who go on adventures to defend cities, slay monsters, and fulfill other challenges. Heroes had an essential role in ancient Greek society. They were often connected with certain towns, and the inhabitants of such cities treated them as deities and offered sacrifices to them (and they were often the half-mortal children of gods).

The warriors who participated in the Trojan War are mentioned in the Iliad and the Odyssey, both of which were authored by Homer. These are two epic poems, which are the length of novels and were composed between 800 and 700 BCE. We don't know whether Homer lived; it's possible that several different poets assembled the works over many decades. What we do know, however, is that these writings provide a more in-depth view of the ancient world than any of the other myths do. The characters (Paris, Agamemnon, Achilles, and Odysseus) are in a class by themselves because they did not originate in folktales that were passed down from generation to generation but rather in epic poems that were written about particular stories that the ancient Greeks, for the most part, believed to be historical. Even though they are referred to as heroes, not all act heroically. You will come across spoilt princes, a deadly warlord, and a very flawed individual desperately looking for his home.

6.1 Semele: A Princess of Thebes; Daughter of Cadmus and Harmonia

Princess Semele was the daughter of Thebes' founders, Cadmus and Harmonia, and she had the title of princess in Thebes. Semele was the first of the couple's progeny to meet a sad end brought on by the curse cast upon the family (for more information on the curse, see Cadmus's section). Further instances of the curse placed on the family of Cadmus and

Harmonia include Semele's nephews Actaeon and Pentheus (for more information on Pentheus, see the section for Dionysus), as well as the well-known Oedipus. Surprisingly, Cadmus and Harmonia were unaffected by the curse; the only effect it had on them was the knowledge that it would harm their children and grandchildren.

As the mother of Dionysus, Semele was not only one of the few mortal women to become pregnant with a god after having sexual relations with Zeus (or any other Olympian!), but she was also the only mortal woman to give birth to a god who was as influential and influential as Dionysus. Semele gave birth to Dionysus. The webcomic Lore Olympus covers some events during the time of Zeus and Semele.

Even though Zeus killed their sister Semele, Euripides' play The Bacchae starts with Semele's sisters denying that Zeus was the father of her child. This is despite Semele's death at the deity's hands. The fact that they would not trust Semele even after she had passed away is another consequence of the curse that has been placed on their family.

6.2 Io: A Princess of Argos

Io, the Princess of Argos, was known for her beauty. She performed the duties of a priestess at the Hera temple (Argos is the city most beloved by the goddess Hera). At some point in the future, Io will be referred to by some people as the Egyptian goddess Isis. As a result of the proximity of many civilizations surrounding the Mediterranean, gods and goddesses often appeared in more than one culture. This allowed people to recognize their deities in the pantheons of other nations. In certain cultures, Io was considered to be the personification of the moon.

In the film Clash of the Titans from 2010, there is a character that goes by the name of Io; nevertheless, even though she has certain qualities in common with the real Io, she is not the same Io. Io was a character in the ancient Greek drama Prometheus Bound, which Aeschylus wrote. In this play, Io's wanderings brought her into contact with the Titan Prometheus as he was being held captive in his eternal punishment.

Io's travels took her to Egypt, and it was there, on the Nile banks, that she could finally escape the gadfly's clutches forever. The ancient Greeks believed that her offspring had governed that region for many years. Some people believe that this is how she came to be linked with the Egyptian goddess Isis, who at the time would have already been well-known across the area as a goddess in her own right.

6.3 Europa: A Phoenician Princess

Phoenicia was an ancient civilization located on the coast of the Mediterranean Sea in what is now the Middle East. Europa was a young lady from that society (in modern-day Lebanon and beyond). The ancient Greeks counted the Phoenicians as one of their most important commercial partners. Eventually, the Phoenicians spread their colonial towns across the Middle East and northern Africa (the famous city of Carthage began as a Phoenician colony). Europa was a princess who lived in the city of Tyre. She was the daughter of the king and queen of Tyre, and she had two brothers named Phoenix and Cadmus.

According to legend, the European continent got its name from the mythical figure called Europa. It was the continent of her nightmares that sought to abduct her with Zeus's help behind them. It is not a very pleasant tale, but it is the first of many dramatic tales, including bulls and the island of Crete. These tales are told to explain how Europe earned its name.

6.4 Leda: A Queen of Sparta; Mother of Castor, Polydeuces, Helen, and Clytemnestra

Leda was the queen of Sparta. She married Tyndareus, the king of Sparta, and was the mother of four sets of twins: Castor and Polydeuces, Helen and Clytemnestra, and Clytemnestra and Helen. She is most well known for appearing in several works of art with Zeus, who often takes the shape of a swan in these depictions. One of the most ingenious methods that Zeus impregnated a human with notably godly offspring was by disguising himself as a swan to be with a lady and have sexual relations with her. As a result of this one-of-a-kind circumstance, it is normally quite simple to recognize Leda in ancient iconography.

There is much room for interpretation regarding which of Leda's children were fathered by Zeus and which were fathered by her husband, Tyndareus. The same is true when determining who was born from an egg or which children were born at the same time in which egg. It is generally accepted that although Castor and Polydeuces were identical twins, Helen and Polydeuces were the ones who were blessed with miraculous births.

6.5 Actaeon: A Shepherd and Hunter of Boeotia

Actaeon was a young man and an accomplished hunter. He was born in the province of Boeotia to his parents, Autono and Aristaeus. It is believed that Cadmus and Harmonia, the first settlers of Thebes and the parents of Autono, were his ancestors. Because of this connection, Actaeon's destiny was a direct outcome of the affliction placed on that family (see the entries on Cadmus, Semele, Oedipus, and Dionysus). The life of Cadmus and Harmonia's family was filled with many heartbreaking events.

Although Cadmus and Harmonia's immediate family saw a great deal of tragedy, the pair were never directly affected by it. Nothing especially unfortunate occurred to them, yet their children, grandchildren, and even ancestors farther back in their family tree endured some of the most terrible endings in Greek mythology. Actaeon is among the most well-known instances of this.

6.6 Theseus: A Hero and Prince of Athens

Theseus was an Athenian hero credited with being one of the city-first state's monarchs (but first, he was a prince of Athens). The people of Athens revered him because they believed he was their city's original creator. You may be familiar with the name Theseus because of the movie Immortals; however, the representation of Theseus in that film doesn't have much in common with the genuine tale.

Theseus was the son of Aegeus, but it's possible that Poseidon was his biological father as well. Aegeus had been attempting to have a child since he was the King of Athens and needed an heir, but neither of the two ladies he had married was able to become pregnant by him. He eventually gave up trying to have a kid. In the end, he traveled to the Oracle, and after some time, he found himself in the city of Troezen, where he had a sexual encounter with his friend's daughter, Aethra (who was also with Poseidon on the same night, hence the confusion). Aegeus went back to Athens, while Aethra remained in Troezen. Eventually, Aethra became pregnant and gave birth to a boy named Theseus.

Theseus ran into "bandits" on his way from Troezen to Athens, where he was planning to meet up with his father. Troezen is where Theseus' journey began. By the time he arrived in Athens, he already had a string of murders under his belt. According to legend, Theseus had already taken the lives of many individuals who had committed murder themselves. Theseus made it a point to execute them in the same manner as they were said to have executed other people. This included bending two trees, tying a guy's feet to one and his arms to the other, and then allowing the trees to return to their original position, which resulted in the man being severed in two.

6.7 Hippolyta: An Amazonian Queen

Although the majority of sources concur that Theseus did indeed meet an Amazonian queen, there is no general agreement as to which Amazonian queen Theseus met; it was either Hippolyta or Antiope (or even another lady completely!). To avoid confusion, we shall refer to the Amazonian queen in the issue as Hippolyta for the rest of this discussion.

Theseus and his friend Pirithous traveled to the land of the Amazons. Pirithous was the same friend who assisted Theseus in kidnapping the famous Helen of Sparta, who later became the queen of Troy (see Leda's entry), and who attempted to assist Theseus in kidnapping Persephone, who was the queen of the Underworld herself. Because of this, he and Pirithous were sentenced to spend some time in the Underworld until Heracles could rescue them. Theseus and Pirithous were pals compelled to get into mischief together at every opportunity.

When they arrived at what was commonly known as Themiscyra, the home of the Amazons, the ladies there greeted them with open arms. The Amazons did not fear men since they were aware of their capabilities and chose to treat them as guests in their city instead. Theseus took advantage of this by having Hippolyta, their queen, bring welcome presents to him on his ship. After she had boarded the ship to distribute these gifts to the guests, Theseus sailed sail and kidnapped the queen. As a result of Theseus's attack on Hippolyta, she got pregnant and gave birth to Hippolytus.

In one version of the narrative of Hippolyta, the hero Heracles is the one who decides what happens to her in the end. The task of recovering Hippolyta's battle belt was included as one of Heracles' infamous Twelve Labors. Ares presented her with the battle belt, and she wore it with pride until Heracles came looking for it. Heracles was after it. Hippolyta did not fear Heracles, like how she did not fear Theseus, so she welcomed him and offered the battle belt to him as a present.

On the other hand, Hera was there while Heracles was doing his labor, and she wreaked havoc in whatever manner she could. She successfully persuaded the other Amazons that Heracles was attempting to abduct their queen, and as a result, they sprang into action to rescue her. When Heracles saw the other ladies coming at him in that manner, he chose to disregard how kind and kind Hippolyta had been toward him, and instead, he chose to murder her. He was successful in his defense against the remaining Amazons and could sail away with the battle belt that Hippolyta had so sweetly and gladly handed to him. Most ancient Greek heroes lacked the more humane features of real heroism, one of its defining characteristics.

Although Hippolyta and the Amazons are among the most well-known figures in mythology, there is surprisingly little material available about them in written form. The Amazonomachy, also known as the conflict with the Amazons, is shown on the west metopes of the Parthenon in Athens. Copies of these depictions may be seen in the Acropolis Museum. The Amazons and their homeland of Themiscyra make appearances in the Wonder Woman comic book series, which has been ongoing for a long time. More recently, in the DC movie Wonder Woman, Hippolyta and Antiope were represented as Diana's aunt and mother (2017). The film was released in 2017.

6.8 Ariadne and Phaedra: Princess of Crete; Goddess and Wife of Dionysus; Wife of Theseus

Princesses of Crete and sisters of several members of the Cretan royal family, including the Minotaur, Ariadne and Phaedra, were the offspring of Pasiphaë and Minos (to him, they were only half-sisters). Ariadne's feelings for Theseus quickly developed when he landed on Crete to take out the Minotaur. He was charming and intriguing, a prince from a land far away named Athens who requested her assistance. Theseus was able to slay the Minotaur, thanks largely to the assistance she provided for him. Theseus would never have made it through if she hadn't been there to supply the thread that guided his route and probably even the sword he used to slay the monster. Without her, he never would have made it.

After Theseus had successfully slain the Minotaur, Ariadne assisted him in evading capture on the island itself, and the two of them eventually made their way to the island of Naxos. When Ariadne was sound asleep, Theseus cast her aside (he did so many terrible things!). Ariadne awakened on an unfamiliar island, having assisted a strange man in the murder of her half-brother and the defiance of her country. She had also left her whole family behind for this guy and found herself unexpectedly alone. She could not believe what Theseus had done to her and how she ended up in this precarious situation. But almost as fast as Theseus had given her up, she was rescued when the deity Dionysus came onto the island with a group of his Maenads. The Maenads were a group of beautiful women who were devoted to Dionysus. Ariadne and Dionysus, the god of wine and revelry, both fell in love after meeting each other for the first time. They wed swiftly and went on to have children; finally, Ariadne was elevated to the status of a goddess and moved to Mount Olympus with Dionysus.

Phaedra became Theseus' wife after he divorced Ariadne and married Phaedra's sister after leaving her on the island of Naxos. This allegedly took place considerably later in his life, which, according to some accounts, makes it somewhat less objectionable. When Theseus was married to Phaedra, the pair traveled to Troezen, where Theseus had spent his childhood. There he had his first meeting with Hippolytus, his son. His son with the Amazonian queen Hippolyta was transferred to Troezen while he was a kid, and it was there that he matured into an amazing young man. He was a talented athlete and rather attractive, but despite these attributes, he chose to worship Artemis rather than the goddess Aphrodite.

The fact that Hippolytus favored Artemis above Aphrodite resulted in Aphrodite placing a curse on him. The curse, however, had a greater impact on Theseus's wife, Hippolytus's wife, than it did on Hippolytus himself. Phaedra became interested in Hippolytus when he was at Troezen. Phaedra realized that she was falling in love with Hippolytus and decided to act on her feelings by expressing them to him. Hippolytus had little interest in love or women, even though he was also his stepmother's biological son. Phaedra's love for him was cursed, so when he turned her down, she felt she had no choice but to take her own life. After discovering the letter that Phaedra had left for herself, Theseus approached Hippolytus and exiled him from Troezen. This tale is related to Euripides's play Hippolytus, considered one of the Greek playwright's most popular works.

6.9 Heracles: A Hero of Thebes; Son of Zeus

Heracles, or Hercules as he was more well-known in Roman and Latin culture, was a hero from ancient Greece. He was one of the most well-known heroes in mythology, and there are a significant number of tales that are connected to him. The name Hercules is derived from the Greek hero Heracles, who the Romans subsequently adopted as one of their most significant heroes. As a result, the name Hercules is now often used. Even though his Greek name is more ancient and more authentic (the Greek Heracles was claimed to have stormed Troy long before even the Trojan War!), he is seldom referred to by that name outside Greek sources. Heracles, the son of Zeus and a human woman called Alcmene, was by far the most powerful and spectacular of all heroes. He was also the most famous. On more than one occasion, Hera has taken vengeance on people who were connected with Zeus, but the affair with Heracles has become legendary.

Hera put much more effort into punishing Heracles than with any of Zeus's many other forays outside of their marriage. Most of the challenges he faced were due to Hera's attempts to destroy him for simply being the son of Zeus. Hera's efforts to destroy Heracles were motivated by the fact that he was Zeus's son.

Hera, who was never going to stop punishing Heracles for the fact that he was her husband's son, was the one who drove Eurystheus. Therefore, Eurystheus gave Heracles a task list of twelve labors, each of which was difficult for the majority of previous heroes:

1. Heracles was tasked with killing the impenetrable Nemean Lion (see Typhon and Echidna's entry) in The First Labor. Fortunately, Heracles's strength enabled him to strangle the lion rather than penetrate it.

2. The Second Labor: He had to slay the Lernean Hydra, a monster with many heads that developed two new ones whenever one was eliminated! Each time Heracles severed one of the heads, two more sprouted in its place. Heracles was eventually able to cauterize each neck after removing the head, stopping regrowth.

3. Heracles was tasked with bringing back a deer with golden antlers that were holy to Artemis. It took him a whole year (!), but he was ultimately successful.

4. Heracles was tasked with capturing the Erymanthian Hog, a monster boar that terrorized the land. Hercules captured it.

5. Heracles was ordered to clean the Augean Stables in one day as part of the Fifth Labor (a very different sort of labor). Heracles had to divert a couple of rivers and flood these stables to clean them since they had not been cleaned for decades.

6. The Sixth Labor: Heracles chased away the Stymphalian Birds, a troublesome band of birds. Athena assisted him in this endeavor.

7. He had to capture the Cretan Bull (see the page for Pasiphaë and Minos). He successfully released the bull at Marathon, known as the Marathonian Bull, which Theseus eventually caught.

8. The eighth labor required Heracles to catch Diomedes' man-eating horses. This was straightforward; he killed Diomedes and took the horses.

9. Heracles was instructed to return the war belt of Hippolyta, queen of the Amazons, for his ninth labor.

10. Heracles seized the Cattle of Geryon, a creature with three bodies, during his tenth labor.

11. The Eleventh Labor: This one was challenging. Heracles was to deliver the golden apples of the Hesperides to Eurystheus, but he had no idea where to locate them. Heracles went and ultimately located the Titan Atlas, the father of the Hesperides, who assisted him in obtaining the apples. Atlas was renowned for holding the sky on his shoulders, while art depicts him carrying the earth.

12. Heracles had to collect Cerberus from the Underworld, where he also rescued Theseus for his twelfth and last labor.

Even after completing the Twelve Labors, Heracles could not find rest or tranquility. He married Hebe, the goddess of youth and daughter of Hera and Zeus.

6.10 Perseus: A Hero; Son of Zeus

Perseus was a legendary figure in Greek mythology. Perseus was conceived in one of the most remarkable and fascinating episodes in all of Greek mythology, which is often omitted from depictions of mythology in popular culture. Zeus appeared to the mother of Perseus, Dana, as a shower of gold. It was sufficient for her to get pregnant with Perseus.

Acrisius imprisoned his daughter, Dana. The Oracle informed Acrisius that Dana's son would overthrow him, so he imprisoned Dana to prevent this from occurring. But Zeus (the eternal tyrant) felt compelled to be with Dana (it is doubtful she felt the same), so he came to her as the aforementioned gold rain.

In the end, Perseus and his mother fled Acrisius, but this did not resolve their issues. They arrived at a country controlled by Polydectes, who wanted to marry Dana. Polydectes was significantly more troublesome than Zeus but was far less amusing (he didn't emerge as a shower of money!). Polydectes' efforts to have Perseus murdered so he could be with Dana resulted in some heroic adventures for Perseus, which was fortunate from a narrative standpoint.

Although Hercules and Perseus rode Pegasus in the Disney film Hercules and in Clash of the Titans, Pegasus was only ever ridden by Bellerophon. Together, they infamously slew the Chimera, a lion with a goat's head sprouting from its back and a snake's tail.

6.11 Medusa: A Gorgon

Medusa was one of three sisters named Gorgon. Stheno and Euryale were the names of the other two. Only Medusa was mortal among the three daughters of the sea monster Ceto and the sea deity Phorcys. In many early Greek myths, Medusa was a monster born of monsters. However, this is not always the case, and by the time of the Romans, her narrative had evolved and altered. The sisters were often portrayed as winged, snake-covered creatures with massive, snarling fangs that dwelt close to the similarly horrible Graeae, who were also offspring of Phorcys.

According to later legends, Medusa had an entirely different personality. She was still mostly known for her snake-like hair and ability to turn men to stone with a single glance, but she was represented as a lady rather than a monster. In later, more elaborate depictions of Medusa, these characteristics were curses cast upon her. In one of the most tragic tales of ancient mythology, as recorded by the Roman poet Ovid, Medusa was once a beautiful Athena priestess renowned for her luxurious hair. One day, she was at the temple of Athena, worshiping the goddess, when Poseidon happened upon her and became entranced. Like his brother Zeus, Poseidon had the propensity to take whatever woman he desired, so he attacked Medusa. Being a virgin goddess, Athena was angered by this behavior, which occurred in her temple of all places.

She punished Medusa because she could not punish Poseidon, an older and more powerful deity than herself. Athena changed Medusa's gorgeous hair into repulsive snakes, making her turn men to stone with a single glance. Perseus' mission to slay Medusa in this rendition is a far more tragic tale. He did not come to slay a deadly creature but a lady a deity had victimized. Chrysaor and Pegasus, the offspring of Medusa's death, were born due to Poseidon's attack since Poseidon is the horse god. After Perseus used Medusa's head as a weapon, it was put on the goddess Athena's shield, where it appears in most depictions of the deity.

Some see Athena's action not as a punishment but as an attempt to avert more harm to Medusa. Medusa was no longer attractive to predatory men or gods; she could protect herself by turning them to stone. In any case, Ovid's rendition of her narrative is far more sympathetic than the majority of earlier depictions. While this sympathetic view of Medusa is generally attributed to Ovid alone, the early Greek author Hesiod also mentions that Medusa was attacked by Poseidon, making this one of the oldest readings of her narrative.

In ancient Greece and Rome, the figure of a Gorgon, notably the head of Medusa, was employed for protection. This motif was and is particularly significant in Sicily, where a Gorgon appears on the region's flag.

6.12 Jason: A Hero and Prince of Iolchus

Jason was a famous hero for his ship, journey, and wife. He was the captain of the Argo, the vessel on which the Argonauts embarked on their search for the Golden Fleece. Among the Argonauts were Atalanta, Castor and Polydeuces (see Leda's page), Orpheus (see his and Eurydice's entry), Theseus, and even Heracles. These warriors are more well-known than Jason, but his wife, the sorceress Medea, was possibly even more renowned. The narrative of Jason, Medea, and the Argonauts is depicted in the 1963 film Jason and the Argonauts, which is most notable for its stop-motion skeletons.

Mythologically, Jason was the lawful ruler of Iolchus, but his father was deposed by his uncle and father's brother, Pelias. Jason was kept away as a toddler and returned as an adult without a sandal. Pelias had been warned that a man with one sandal would bring about his downfall, so he was cautious of Jason's return and immediately tried to have him murdered by sending him on a mission to retrieve the legendary Golden Fleece, a sheep with real gold fur.

Even though Jason is a well-known hero, he is not very heroic. Without the Argonauts, he never would have reached Colchis, and without Medea, he would never have survived Aetes' trials, much less returned to Iolchus with the Golden Fleece.

6.13 Medea: A Witch; Daughter of Aeëtes; Granddaughter of the Titan Helios

Aeëtes was the son of the Titan Helios and the brother of Circe. According to at least one legend, her mother may have been the witch Hecate, although this is never entirely established. Regardless matter who her mother was, she was descended from a line of witches. Medea was raised in Colchis, in the kingdom ruled by Aeëtes.

The drama titled after Medea was composed by the ancient Greek tragedian Euripides and is her most enduring legacy (though many other ancient playwrights and poets wrote about her too). The drama is being performed today in different forms. Her name has become linked with mental instability and murder, but her tale is not straightforward. Medea is one of the most complicated figures in Greek mythology, and Euripides' portrayal of her is exemplary of an intriguing, flawed, and sympathetic woman in a culture dominated by male narratives.

Since Medea was from Colchis, she was seen as a non-Greek alien. Even in the ancient world, xenophobia existed, and the Greeks were frequently cautious of foreigners who spoke a language other than Greek. This was a major reason why Jason and the Corinthians treated Medea so cruelly (if she had been Greek, he would not have been able to abandon her since they would have been legally married).

6.14 Cadmus: A Hero; Founder of Thebes; a Prince of the Phoenicians

Cadmus was a prince of Tyre, a Phoenician city. He was Europa's brother, the young lady Zeus abducted in the guise of a bull. Cadmus and Harmonia founded the ancient Greek city of Thebes. His descendants are known as the Cadmeians, and they appear in many of the most renowned Greek myths (see entries on Semele, Dionysus, Actaeon, and Oedipus).

Cadmus and Harmonia seldom, if ever, appear in popular culture; nonetheless, Roberto Calasso wrote a magnificent novelization of Greek stories titled The Marriage of Cadmus and Harmony.

According to his legend, Cadmus delivered the alphabet from Phoenicia to the Greek world. The majority of Greek mythology attributes the invention of the ancient Greek alphabet to Cadmus. Historically, the Phoenicians founded settlements across northern Africa, notably the future metropolis of Carthage. The Carthaginians were one of ancient Rome's greatest adversaries and are mentioned in the Aeneid, the account of Rome's origin.

6.15 Atalanta: A Heroine of Arcadia

Atalanta is the sole official heroine (to the degree that any hero was official!) of ancient Greece, i.e., the only woman classified as a hero by the same criteria as Perseus, Hercules, etc. Indeed, there are other strong, independent, and courageous women in Greek mythology, but she is the only one to have earned the title of "heroine."

According to the version, Atalanta was born in either Arcadia or Boeotia to either one pair of parents or another. According to some legends, two ladies called Atalanta had virtually identical lives, although it is more possible that there were two versions of her, probably because two areas desired to claim her as their own.

Irrespective of where Atalanta was born or who her parents were, legend has it that her father was very upset when she was born a girl rather than a boy. He was so disheartened that he abandoned her outdoors to perish in the elements. Yet, instead of dying, she was discovered and nursed by a bear. Her upbringing made her courageous, powerful, and proficient with a bow and arrow.

When Meleager was born, the Fates informed his mother that he would die as soon as a certain piece of wood (which she had just tossed into the fire!) was completely consumed. His mother promptly removed the wood from the fire, bathed it with water, and concealed it for safety. But after Meleager murdered his siblings in the name of a lady, his mother was so enraged that she recovered the concealed wood and threw it into the fire. Meleager dropped lifeless to the ground after it had completely burnt up.

6.16 Daedalus: An Inventor from Athens

Daedalus was an Athens-born inventor descending from the city's first monarchs. He was the most renowned inventor in Greek mythology, famed for his abilities and capacity to construct practically anything (both brilliant, ingenious inventions and super weird ones).

Daedalus appears in the Disney television series Hercules as the father of Hercules' closest buddy, Icarus (Icarus calls Daedalus "Dad-alus"). Moreover, the father and son are shown repeatedly in artwork, lyrics, and literature, typically concerning the tragic fall of Icarus.

Athena was there when Daedalus pushed Talos from the cliff at Athens. When the kid plummeted, she resolved to save him in any way possible. Before he touched the ground, she converted Talos into a partridge. The ancient Greeks thought that Talos' fear of heights caused the partridge to stay grounded and unable to fly like other birds.

6.17 Icarus: The Son of Daedalus

Icarus was imprisoned with his father, Daedalus when Minos punished Daedalus for his part in Pasiphaë's romance with Poseidon's bull. It is unclear what happened to Icarus' mother, Naucrate, during this period since she was not there when he and Daedalus were locked in the Labyrinth, which was Daedalus' design. Even Daedalus could not escape his invention, and only with Pasiphaë's assistance could the two escape. Pasiphaë felt sorry for Daedalus' punishment, as he had been following her directions, so she released them and permitted them to plot their escape from the island of Crete while they hid.

Daedalus set out to identify the most efficient method for them to leave the island and reach the mainland. They could not steal a ship since Minos's fleet was very well-protected, and they would never be able to steal one without anybody noticing. Daedalus judged that the only alternative was flight. They would need to discover a means to leave the island through flight.

Daedalus started constructing wings for himself and his kid. Initially, he imitated the skeletons of the bigger birds he could see on the island by fashioning a skeleton out of wood. The skeleton was adorned with feathers. The wings had to be identical to a bird's, or else they wouldn't operate. He combed the area for feathers of the exact proper size. Everything was meticulously planned: Daedalus could firmly stitch the bigger feathers onto the skeleton, but he attached the tiny feathers using wax since they were too small to sew.

The wings were finally complete. Daedalus instructed Icarus on how to utilize the wings, including how to flap them and how frequently; he emphasized that Icarus must not fly so close to the sea that the wings were wet since this would damage the wings and force Icarus to fall to his death. He also advised

Icarus not to soar too high since if he went too near the sun, the wax keeping the tiny feathers in place would melt, and he would fall to his death again. After determining the rules and regulations, Daedalus connected his son's wings, followed by his own, and they took flight.

They flew nicely for a while; the wings performed as intended. The longer they flew, though, the more restless Icarus became. Despite his youth, the steady flapping and straight flight were becoming monotonous. Icarus wanted to have fun, so he altered his flying path to make the voyage more thrilling. His father reprimanded his kid for taking the risk. However, Icarus was obstinate, and he continued to enjoy flying, going lower and higher. He felt invincible and confident in his abilities. But before long, he flew too near to the sun and too high. Icarus fell once the wax on his wings started to melt, exactly as Daedalus had foretold. Icarus cried out for his father before falling into the water and dying. Daedalus wept for his son and buried his remains on the nearest island before he could move on to Sicily via flying.

6.18 Pasiphaë and Minos: A Queen and King of Knossos, Crete

On the island of Crete, the palace of Knossos was ruled over by Pasiphaë and Minos, respectively. Her father, Helios, was a Titan and the god of the sun, and her mother, Perseis, was a nymph. Pasiphaë was their daughter. Zeus and Europa gave birth to Minos, who was their son. The presence of the Minotaur, a monster that was half human and half bull, became synonymous with their rule over Crete. The beast made its home inside Daedalus's infamous Labyrinth, which he constructed, and would sometimes gorge itself on unfortunate parties of young Athenians.

Madeline Miller's book Circe is a visceral retelling of the birth of the Minotaur. Pasiphaë appears in the tale as the sister of the witch goddess Circe. After his death, Minos was elevated to judge in the underworld.

6.19 Minotaur: A Monstrous Half-Man, Half Bull

The Minotaur was the offspring of Pasipha's forced love affair with Poseidon's bull and Minos' refusal to fulfill his pledge to sacrifice the bull. Asterius (or Asterion) was the Minotaur's name, meaning "the starry one." As soon as the Minotaur was born, people around him recognized he needed to be controlled. Although many mythological half-human monsters have human traits, the Minotaur is terrible and cruel. In contrast to many other half-human creatures, the Minotaur's upper half was a bull (or occasionally only the head, in which case he had extremely human abs!), and he did not seem to have preserved any human cognition: no thoughts, emotions, or empathy. Simply put, he was a monster.

While the Minotaur is purely mythical, Bronze Age Cretans (one of the first Greek civilizations) used bull symbolism extensively. There were paintings of bulls everywhere and depictions of Cretan youth jumping over bulls.

Minos and Pasipha feared the Minotaur's wrath so much that they had Daedalus design a containment system for him. Daedalus constructed the Labyrinth so that the Minotaur could live apart from the Cretan people while receiving regular nourishment. Even the inventor of the Labyrinth, Daedalus, could not find his way out of it. It also helped to conceal the Minotaur, therefore concealing Minos's disgrace.

In this era, Minos waged war against Athens and was ready to utterly destroy the city. Instead, the parties reached an understanding: Minos would relent, and the Athenians would send seven young men and seven young women to Crete every seven years. These adolescents would fall prey to the Minotaur.

The Minotaur was ultimately destroyed only when Theseus, a prince of Athens, agreed to be one of these Athenian boys. Theseus sailed to Crete as one of its captives, seduced Ariadne, the princess of Crete, and persuaded her to assist him. Ariadne provided Theseus with a thread to help him navigate the Labyrinth and find the Minotaur. After slaying the creature, he could retrace his steps and exit the Labyrinth, something that had not been possible for anybody else who had entered it.

6.20 Orpheus and Eurydice: A Young Musician and a Beautiful Young Woman

Orpheus was the son of a Thracian monarch and the muse Calliope. He was a young man from Thrace. Orpheus took after his mother and was regarded as the greatest poet and musician among mortals (second only to the gods!). Everyone within hearing distance was captivated by his music and, by extension, by him as he played the lyre. He could command anyone's attention with a single note. Orpheus participated in the search for the Golden Fleece, assisting Jason and the Argonauts with his musical abilities.

While Orpheus was aboard the Argo, he protected the other sailors from the Sirens' luring songs. As they sang their enticing melody, Orpheus played his lyre so loudly and brilliantly that he drowned out the Sirens' singing, which would have otherwise doomed the ship and its crew.

Orpheus wed Eurydice, a young lady. Unfortunately, we don't know much about her other than that he loved her very much, and based on their narrative, we may presume she loved him as well.

During the ages of the ancient world, Orpheus's personality altered tremendously. Eventually, an Orphic Tradition emerged, consisting of religious ceremonies centered on Orpheus that reconstructed the genesis of the gods and mythology as a whole.

Conclusion

Although the Greek myths were first recounted thousands of years ago, we still consider them a vital part of our existence. The way that people understand them now is much different from when they were originally penned.

At one point, myths were also used to explain natural occurrences such as earthquakes and lightning. When the ancient Greeks gained greater knowledge about science, they discovered additional explanations for natural events. Because of this, myths began to seem less significant or credible as explanations.

Despite this, myths continue to be significant because they relate tales about things that happen to everyone and feel that everyone has. Modern people still experience emotions such as rage, love, and envy, just as the ancient Greeks did. In addition to being thrilling and action-packed with excitement and adventure, the myths are fantastic tales.

For millennia, creative types have looked to the Greek mythos for ideas to include in their works of art and writing. They depicted events from the myths in paintings and based plays on the Greeks' oral storytelling traditions. Myths have inspired operas composed by composers, while contemporary novelists have repeated the tales they tell.

Greek mythology remains an integral element of our culture and society even now.

Greek mythology is the source of well-known idioms, including "Pandora's box." The myth of Pandora serves as a cautionary tale to remind people to be cautious about their choices since their acts might have severe repercussions. The exploits of Heracles have been adapted into many mediums, including film, television, and computer and console games. Clash of the Titans (1981) and Troy are two movies based on Greek tales (2004).

In addition, figures from Greek mythology have been adapted for marketing. 1 The image of the Greek deity Hermes, complete with his winged crown and shoes, is often employed by delivery services such as FTD, which is a firm that specializes in the delivery of flowers.

From the beginning of civilization, Greek myths have been passed down from generation to generation by oral tradition. These accounts of thrilling moments and intense feelings are destined to be told for many years.

Made in United States
Orlando, FL
23 May 2023